This Book Belongs To

_____

ANGELS

Ariel Books

Andrews and McMeel
Kansas City

ISBN: 0-8362-3042-6

Library of Congress Number: 92-75639

Marbleized endpapers © 1985 by Katherine Radcliffe

Introduction

Angels have beguiled and enchanted us since ancient times. Some archaeologists date the first depiction of an angel to Babylon, between 2500 and 1000 B.C. Others argue for earlier dates, citing possible angels in the Egyptian pantheon of gods and winged creatures carved in rock found in Mesopotamia and Assyria. Scholars have considered Hermes, the Greek god and messenger between earth and heaven, to be an angel, and indeed the word ANGEL in Greek means "messenger."

But if angels are old, they are also young —as recent as the last sighting. Books have been written about encounters with angels in the here and now, and as a poetic image—as you will see in this book—they are as enduring as the concept of God.

What is an angel? Angels have been described as watchers, servants, holy ones, and even sons of God. In Judeo-Christianity the angels were ordered and ranked and given a host of names that indicated their place in angelic hierarchy: cherubim, seraphim, and archangels, to note a few. The earliest angels, even the ones in the Old Testament, did not have wings. The ladder Jacob witnessed had on it angels climbing down from heaven. In another of the early books of the Bible, angels visit with Abraham as if they were ordinary humans; they even dine with him.

What remains constant in every account of angels, from ancient days to the present, is that they are both messengers and companions to humans, sent from a realm beyond the earth. In every great book of belief and devotion, in the highest art forms known to us, angels appear and, in one way or another, help us, advise us, inspire us, or amaze us.

In the quotations and verses in this book, the many facets of angels are illuminated. As they take wing in your heart, you will see that these celestial friends have not deserted us.

A NGELS

$\mathcal{A}$ NGELS

*Had he looked up he might have seen angels
of light dancing above the throbbing bright
squares—in whirlwinds, will-o'-the-wisps,
and golden eddies—but he didn't look up, for
. . . he had seen angels many times before.
Their faces shone from paintings; their voices
rode the long and lovely notes of arias; they
descended to capture the bodies and souls of
young children; they sang and perched in the
trees; they were in the surf and the streams;
they inspired dancing; and they were the right
and holy combination of words in poetry.*

— MARK HELPRIN
A Soldier of the Great War

It is only with the heart that one can see rightly; what is essential is invisible to the eye.

—ANTOINE DE SAINT-EXUPERY
The Little Prince

That's all an angel is, an idea of God.

— MEISTER ECKHART

Angels and ministers of grace defend us.

— WILLIAM SHAKESPEARE
Hamlet, I. iv

$\mathcal{A}$ NGELS

*So many wings come here
dipping honey
and speak here
in your home Oh
God.*

—AZTEC POEM

I looked over Jordan and what did I see?
Comin' for to carry me home
A band of angels, comin' after me,
Comin' for to carry me home.

— **AFRICAN-AMERICAN SPIRITUAL**
Swing Low, Sweet Chariot

Their garments are white, but with an unearthly whiteness. I cannot describe it, because it cannot be compared to earthly whiteness; it is much softer to the eye. These bright Angels are enveloped in a light so different from ours that by comparison everything else seems dark. When you see a band of fifty, you are lost in amazement. They seem clothed with golden plates, constantly moving, like so many suns.

—PERE LAMY

I believe we are free, within limits, and yet there is an unseen hand, a guiding angel, that somehow, like a submerged propeller, drives us on.

—RABINDRANATH TAGORE

For He shall give His angels charge over thee, to keep thee in all thy ways. They shall bear thee up in their hands, lest thou dash thy foot against a stone.

—PSALMS 91:11, 12

$\mathcal{A}$ NGELS

Angels can fly because they take themselves lightly.

—SCOTTISH SAYING

The angels keep their ancient places
Turn but a stone and start a wing!
'Tis ye, 'tis ye, your estranged faces
That miss the many-splendoured thing.

—**FRANCIS THOMPSON**
The Kingdom of God

Still an angel appear to each lover beside,
But still be a woman to you.

—**THOMAS PARNELL**
When Thy Beauty Appears

The golden hours on angel wings
Flew o'er me and my dearie;
For dear to me as light and life
Was my sweet Highland Mary.

—ROBERT BURNS
Highland Mary

If I have freedom in my love,
And in my soul am free,
Angels alone that soar above
Enjoy such liberty.

—RICHARD LOVELACE
To Althea: From Prison

29

At the round earth's imagin'd corners, blow
Your trumpets, angels, and arise, arise
From death, you numberless infinities
Of souls.

—JOHN DONNE
Holy Sonnets

Our acts our angels are, or good or ill,
Our fatal shadows that walk by still.

—JOHN FLETCHER
The Honest Man's Fortune

He shall cover thee with his feathers, and
under his wings shalt thou trust: his truth
shall be thy shield and buckler.

—PSALM 91:4

*Yet I am the necessary angel of
   earth,
Since, in my sight, you see the earth again . . .*

— **WALLACE STEVENS**
Angel Surrounded by Paysans

"Hey, angel," Amarante called out in his dream. "What's a rainbow doing over our town on a sunny day like today?"

... "Maybe it's because for once in your lives you people are trying to do something right."

Abruptly the angel disappeared.

—JOHN NICHOLS
The Milagro Beanfield War

$\mathcal{A}$ NGELS

Twice or thrice had I loved thee,
Before I knew thy face or name;
So in a voice, so in a shapeless flame,
Angels affect us oft, and worshipped be . . .

—JOHN DONNE
Air and Angels

Maybe other angels have dropped into other Elm Street backyards? Behind fences, did neighbors help earlier hurt ones? Folks keep so much of the best stuff quiet, don't they.

— **ALLAN GURGANUS**
It Had Wings

$\mathscr{A}$ NGELS

Be not forgetful to entertain strangers, for thereby some have entertained angels unawares.

—Hebrews 13:2

And yet, as angels in some brighter dreams
Call to the soul when man doth sleep,
So some strange thoughts transcend our
    wonted themes,
And into glory peep.

—HENRY VAUGHAN
They Are All Gone

*Outside the open window
The morning air is all awash with angels.*

—RICHARD WILBUR
*Love Calls Us to the Things
of This World*

$\mathcal{A}$ NGELS

$\mathcal{A}$ N G E L S

Angels descending, bringing
from above,
Echoes of mercy, whispers of
love.

—FANNY J. CROSBY
Blessed Assurance

Unless you can love, as the angels may
With the breadth of heaven betwixt you;
Unless you can dream that his faith is fast,
Through behoving and unbehoving;
Unless you can die when the dream is past—
Oh, never call it loving!

—ROBERT BROWNING
A Woman's Shortcomings

It is wonderful that every angel, in whatever direction he turns his body and face, sees the Lord in front of him.

—EMMANUEL SWEDENBORG
The True Christian Religion

Bless the Lord, ye his angels, that excel in strength, that do his commandments, hearkening unto the voice of his word.

—Psalms, 103:20

Look homeward Angel now . . .

—JOHN MILTON
Lycidas

All God's angels come to us disguised.

—JAMES RUSSELL LOWELL
On the Death of a Friend's Child

ANGELS

Angels, we have heard on high
Singing sweetly through the night,
And the mountains in reply
Echoing their brave delight.

— FRENCH CHRISTMAS CAROL

The angels sing the praise of their Lord and ask forgiveness for those on earth....

—THE KORAN XLII:5

It is not because angels are holier than men or devils that makes them angels, but because they do not expect holiness from another, but from God alone.

—WILLIAM BLAKE

We trust in plumed procession
For such the angels go—
Rank after Rank, with even feet—
And uniforms of Snow.

—EMILY DICKINSON
To Fight Aloud, Is Very Brave

Good-night, sweet prince,
And flights of angels sing thee to thy rest!

—WILLIAM SHAKESPEARE
Hamlet, V. ii

Hold the fleet angel fast until he bless thee.

—NATHANIEL COTTON
Tomorrow

And now were these two men, as 'twere, in Heaven.... Being swallowed up with the sight of angels, and with hearing of their melodious notes.

—JOHN BUNYAN
The Pilgrim's Progress

$\mathcal{A}$ N G E L S

$\mathcal{A}$ NGELS

Matthew, Mark, Luke and John.
The bed be blest that I lie on.
Four angels to my bed,
Four angels round my head,
One to watch, and one to pray,
And two to bear my soul away.

—THOMAS ADY
A Candle in the Dark

. . . all in bright array
The Cherubim descended; on the ground
Gliding meteorous, as Ev'ning Mist
Ris'n from a River o'er the marish glides,
And gathers ground fast at the Laborer's heel
Homeward returning.

—JOHN MILTON
Paradise Lost, XII

Hush! my dear, lie still and slumber,
Holy angels guard thy bed!
Heavenly blessing without number
Gently falling on thy head.

—ISAAC WATTS
Divine Songs

It is said by those who ought to understand such things, that the good people, or the fairies, are some of the angels who were turned out of heaven, and who landed on their feet in this world, while the rest of their companions, who had more sin to sink them, went down farther to a worse place.

—WILLIAM BUTLER YEATS
Fairy Tales of Ireland

$\mathcal{A}$ NGELS

How like an angel came I down!
How Bright are all things here!
When first among his works I did appear,
Oh, how their glory did me crown!

—THOMAS TRAHERNE
Wonder

And now it is an angel's song,
That makes the heavens be mute.

—SAMUEL TAYLOR COLERIDGE
The Rime of the Ancient Mariner

Like living flame their faces seemed to
  glow.
Their wings were gold. And all
  their bodies shone
more dazzling white than any
  earthly show.

—DANTE
  The Paradiso, Canto XXXI
  (John Ciardi trans.)

Angels

*Look how the floor of heaven
Is thick inlaid with patterns of bright gold.
There's not the smallest orb which thou
    behold'st
But in his motion like an angel sings,
Still quiring to the young-ey'd cherubins.*

—WILLIAM SHAKESPEARE
The Merchant of Venice

ℋ NGELS

$\mathcal{A}$ NGELS

The angels laughed. God looked down from his seventh heaven and smiled. The angels spread their wings and, together with Elijah, flew upward into the sky.

—ISAAC BASHEVIS SINGER
Elijah the Slave

Everyone entrusted with a mission is an angel. ...All forces that reside in the body are angels.

—MOSES MAIMONIDES

The text of this book was set in
Gavotti Script and Bodoni
by Dix Type Inc. of Syracuse, New York

Book design by Maura Fadden Rosenthal

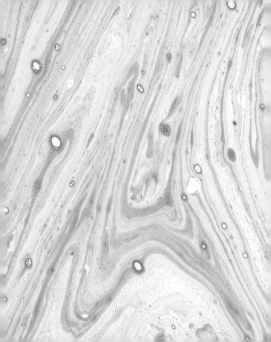